Anatomy of a Scandal

THE RECORDER;

PRINTED BY HENRY PACE, & JAMES T. CALLENDER. RICHMOND, VIRGINIA;
PUBLISHED EVERY WEDNESDAY AND SATURDAY. SUBSCRIPTION FOUR DOLLARS PER ANNUM, IN ADVANCE.

THE PRESIDENT
AGAIN.

IT is well known, that the man, *whom it delighteth the people to honor*, keeps, and for many years past has kept, as his concubine, one of his own slaves. Her name is SALLY. The name of her eldest son is TOM. His features are said to bear a striking although sable resemblance to those of the president himself. The boy is ten or twelve years of age. His mother went to France in the same vessel with Mr. Jefferson and his two daughters. The delicacy of this arrangement must strike every person of common sensibility. What a sublime pattern for an American ambassador to place before the eyes of two young ladies!

If the reader does not feel himself *disposed to pause* we beg leave to proceed. Some years ago, this story had once or twice been hinted at in *Rind's Federalist*. At that time, we believed the surmise to be an absolute calumny. One reason for thinking so was this. A vast body of people wished to debar Mr. Jefferson from the presidency. The establishment of this SINGLE FACT would have rendered his election impossible. We reasoned thus; that if the allegation had been true, it was sure to have been ascertained and advertised by his enemies, in every corner of the continent. The suppression of so decisive an enquiry serves to shew that the common sense of the federal party was overruled by divine providence. It was the predestination of the supreme being that they should be turned out; that they should be expelled from office by the popula-

Callender's column, September 1, 1802

Richmond Recorder, September 1, 1802

Anatomy of a Scandal

Thomas Jefferson & the SALLY Story

By
Rebecca L. McMurry and James F. McMurry, Jr.

With a foreword by David N. Mayer

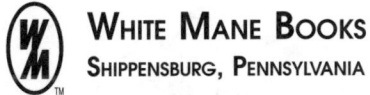

WHITE MANE BOOKS
SHIPPENSBURG, PENNSYLVANIA

Copyright © 2002 by Rebecca L. McMurry and James F. McMurry, Jr.

ALL RIGHTS RESERVED—No part of this book may be reproduced in any form without permission in writing from the publisher, except by a reviewer who wishes to quote brief passages in connection with a review.

This White Mane Books publication
was printed by
Beidel Printing House, Inc.
63 West Burd Street
Shippensburg, PA 17257-0708 USA

The acid-free paper used in this book meets the guidelines for permanence and durability of the Committee on Production Guidelines for Book Longevity of the Council on Library Resources.

For a complete list of available publications
please write
White Mane Books
Division of White Mane Publishing Company, Inc.
P.O. Box 708
Shippensburg, PA 17257-0708 USA

Library of Congress Cataloging-in-Publication Data

McMurry, Rebecca L., 1949-
  Anatomy of a scandal : Thomas Jefferson & the Sally story / by Rebecca L. McMurry and James F. McMurry, Jr.; with a foreword by David N. Mayer.
    p. cm.
  Includes bibliographical references (p.) and index.
  ISBN 1-57249-303-8 (alk. paper)
  1. Jefferson, Thomas, 1743-1826--Relations with women. 2. Jefferson, Thomas, 1743-1826--Relations with slaves. 3. Hemings, Sally. I. McMurry, James F., 1940- II. Title.

E332.2 .M44 2002
973.4'6'092--dc21
[B]   2002016764

PRINTED IN THE UNITED STATES OF AMERICA

To
Herbert Barger,
*Who first conceived of a thorough and unbiased
reexamination of all the historical material by a blue-ribbon
Scholars Commission of professional historians,*

And to
Thomas Jefferson,
For his faith in the power of ordinary people,

We humbly dedicate this volume.

Contents

List of Illustrations		ix
Foreword		xi
Preface		xv
Acknowledgments		xix
A Note on Proper Names and Quotations		xxiii
Chronology of the "SALLY" Story and Associated Persons		xxvi
Chapter 1	The 1998 DNA Study	1
Chapter 2	John Wayles, Colonial Scapegoat	11
Chapter 3	The Randolph Debtors	39
Chapter 4	The Wayles Estate	52
Chapter 5	Randolph Revenge	57
Chapter 6	Callender's "SALLY" Story	68
Chapter 7	That "Thomas Turner" Letter of 1805	85
Chapter 8	Politics and Propaganda	98
Chapter 9	1873 and Madison Hemings	110
Chapter 10	History Repeats Itself	127
Appendix 1	Genealogical Investigation of the Wayles Family in England	131
Appendix 2	Letter of John Wayles to Farrell and Jones, August 30, 1766	136
Appendix 3	The "Thomas Turner" Letter of 1805	142
Appendix 4	The 1873 Story of Madison Hemings	149
Appendix 5	Genealogical Investigation of Hemingses in Virginia	156

Appendix 6 Defending the Legend of "SALLY"	167
Notes	173
Bibliography	189
Index	197

Illustrations

Callender's column, September 1, 1802 .... frontispiece
1. Map of Tidewater Virginia xxiv
2. Randolph family tree xxv
3. Cumberland Tavern crime scene 12
4. Gaol in Williamsburg 14
5. Colonel Chiswell's townhouse in Williamsburg 14
6. Cartouche from Fry-Jefferson map 18
7. Excerpts from John Wayles's letter to Farrell and Jones 24
8. Charles City Courthouse 25
9. Westover Church 29
10. Tuckahoe plantation house 42
11. Tuckahoe school house 44
12. Curles Plantation 44
13. Turkey Island Plantation 45
14. Ryland Randolph's Flood Monument 45
15. Montage of Thomas Jefferson's letter to Farrell
    and Jones 54
16. David Meade Randolph's "Moldavia" 64
17. Auction announcement in *Richmond Enquirer* 67
18. Meriwether Jones's article in *Richmond Examiner* 78
19. David Meade Randolph and his wife, Mary 80
20. Thomas Jefferson and John Wayles Eppes 81
21. "Thomas Turner" letter, June 19, 1805 88
22. "Thomas Turner" letter, October 26, 1805 93

23.	William Wells Brown	102
24.	Thomas Jefferson Randolph	104
25.	Thomas Nast cartoon	105
26.	Map of Ohio counties	107
27.	Madison Hemings's and John Hemings's registrations as free blacks	111
28.	Ludwell Coles's, Eston Hemings's, Robert Scott's, and Burwell Colbert's registrations as free blacks	113
29.	Thomas Jefferson Randolph's surety on deed of transfer	113
30.	Excerpt of Callender's article in *Richmond Recorder*, September 1, 1802	121
31.	Manumission of Mary Hemings by Samuel Coleman	123
32.	Map of Lancaster in the 18th century	132
33.	Furness peninsula in the northwest of Lancaster	133
34.	Hobbs Hole as depicted by Sidney King	159
35.	Excerpt of the court proceedings of the inventory of William Hemings	160
36.	Area of the Fry-Jefferson map showing Tappahannock, Prince George County, and Williamsburg	162
37.	Bowler's Wharf on the Rappahannock River	164
38.	"Longfields" area on the north shore of the James River	166

Foreword

For over two hundred years—ever since it was first raised in print by the notorious hatchet journalist James Callender in a Richmond, Virginia, newspaper in 1802—the allegation that Thomas Jefferson fathered the children of his slave Sally Hemings has been a popular American myth. Although many people today erroneously believe that the Jefferson-Hemings paternity claim is historical fact, the persistence of that belief is merely evidence of the power of the myth and of the various social forces that have helped sustain it throughout American history. Personal and political enmity, partisan conflict, and the slavery controversy helped fuel "the Sally story" in the early 19th century. Today, the story is kept alive because other forces, equally political, in American culture and in the history profession have created an atmosphere in which it has become difficult to separate myth from fact.

As a member of a blue-ribbon Scholars Commission which spent the better part of a year, from summer 2000 until April 2001, reinvestigating the Jefferson-Hemings matter, I have learned that the supposed "evidence" supporting the paternity claim truly is quite weak. Proponents of the Jefferson paternity thesis rely largely on three pieces of documentary evidence: the 1802 Callender article; an 1805 letter published in a Boston, Massachusetts, newspaper and attributed to one "Thomas Turner," of Virginia; and an 1873 article in a Pike County, Ohio, newspaper allegedly reporting an interview with Madison Hemings, the second-youngest son of Sally Hemings. Modern retellings of the story—including Fawn Brodie's controversial Jefferson biography as well as the oral tradition claimed by some Hemings descendants—themselves appear to have been based on one or more of these three sources. The only other important "new evidence" cited by proponents of the Jefferson-Hemings thesis have been the results of a 1998 DNA study and a study of the birth patterns of Hemings's children conducted in 1999 by a staff member of the Thomas Jefferson Foundation (Monticello) and published in *William & Mary Quarterly* in January 2000.

The Scholars Commission reviewed thoroughly not only these pieces of evidence but also all other relevant evidence, many pieces of which pointed to some other male relatives of Thomas Jefferson—his nephews, Peter and Samuel Carr, or his brother, Randolph Jefferson, or perhaps one or more of Randolph's sons—as the likely father, or fathers, of Sally Hemings's children. The 13 scholars who signed the commission's final report concluded unanimously that the Jefferson-Hemings paternity claim was "by no means proven"; and all but one of us found the claim unpersuasive, with our views ranging from serious skepticism about the charge to a conviction that it is almost certainly false. We also found that neither the DNA study nor the statistical study printed in *William & Mary Quarterly* pointed to Jefferson, as opposed to his brother Randolph or perhaps one of Randolph's sons, as the father of Hemings's children.

My own conclusion was that the paternity claim was not at all plausible and that the Jefferson-Hemings story is, quite literally, a myth. In my concurring report for the Scholars Commission, I discussed the story in its broader context, what I describe as the "politicization of American history," and concluded that the persistence of the myth today can be explained as a result of the influence of several phenomena—"political correctness," radical multiculturalism, and postmodernism—which, unfortunately, have helped undermine traditional standards for objectivity in historical scholarship.

Foreword

As I noted in the conclusion to my report,

> [Many people] for various reasons, passionately want to believe that Thomas Jefferson fathered Sally Hemings's children. These include some of the descendants of two of Sally Hemings's children who passionately want their families' oral traditions—and for many of them and their supporters, their places in American history—somehow validated by widespread acceptance of the Jefferson paternity thesis as historical fact. But it is not the role of historians to make people feel good about themselves or their family stories; "feel-good" history is not good history. It is, rather, the role of historians to explain the past as best they can, by following objective methodology and the evidence.

For most people, regardless their views of the merits of the Jefferson-Hemings paternity claim, the story begins with James Callender's 1802 newspaper article. Most people also naively have accepted as true the claim that Jefferson's father-in-law, John Wayles, was the father of Sally Hemings (thus making Sally the half-sister of Jefferson's wife, Martha Wayles Skelton)—a paternity claim that in fact is even more questionable than the claim about Sally's children, for it originated as a naked accusation in the 1805 "Thomas Turner" letter. No one has examined the story behind the stories—the origin of the Callender and Turner stories themselves—until now.

In this book Rebecca and James McMurry make a significant contribution to our understanding of the real, historical story behind the Sally Hemings myths. Although they are not professional historians, the McMurrys in fact have bested many of the historians and other professional scholars who have written on this subject, in doing their research thoroughly and carefully, uncovering the true origins of the Sally story. They reveal, for the first time in print, the full chronology of the story—tracing it back to the scandalmongers with whom it originated, men whose enmity toward Jefferson (and his father-in-law, John Wayles) was both personal and political. It is a fascinating story that needs to be told, and this book tells it ably.

David N. Mayer

Professor of Law and History
Capital University
Columbus, Ohio
July 2001

Professor David N. Mayer returned to academic life after a law practice in Washington, D.C. He earned his Ph.D. in history at the University of Virginia in 1988. Author of many articles and contributions, he is best known for his book, The Constitutional Thought of Thomas Jefferson *(University Press of Virginia, 1995).*

Preface

Investigating the "SALLY" story of James T. Callender from 1802 and the Wetmore/Hemings story of 1873 became an irresistable quest for more than two years. Prompted by the November 5, 1998, issue of *Nature* which showed results of Y chromosome DNA studies on descendants of Jeffersons, Hemingses, and Woodsons, we began to probe the old records of Virginia for additional information about these families. Neither of us has a doctorate in history, but we had shared the hobby of genealogical research on our own families separately and together for many years. We also had personal oral history suggesting that Thomas Jefferson's brother, Randolph, was the father of some of Sally Hemings's children.

Initially, we accepted most of the Wetmore/Hemings story of 1873, based on the published interpretations and arguments of others. However, we had found among our own families that oral traditions could be incorrect while still having informational value. The names and nouns were correct in one of our own family stories, but the verbs and adjectives were wrong. Within that family oral history, the story was simply mixed up with different persons supposedly doing different things than shown in further research. Oral traditions within families need to be taken seriously as possibilities, but they must be checked with other data. We present here the results of these investigations and fact-checking.

As information was picked up bit by bit, we were encouraged to continue tugging at threads again and again. Sometimes genealogical research is much like reading a mystery novel—it is hard to put down. The next page or search might solve the puzzle. In the end, two people working simultaneously, with more than a dozen years of genealogical research experience each, could discover the underlying probabilities and begin to tie the story together in a relatively short period of two years.

Historical and genealogical research into the 18th and 19th centuries has become greatly enhanced in Virginia with the efforts of the Virginia State Library in Richmond. Computerized cataloging, microfilms of the old county records, old newspapers, the Colonial Records Project from papers in the British Public Records Office, and a wide selection of books on Virginia and other states, as well as other countries, drastically reduce the time and effort necessary to develop the important leads. Indexed abstracts of courthouse records for the colonial and early federal periods have been prepared by industrious genealogists for many old Virginia counties. These prove invaluable in this type of research. Nonetheless, the transcriptions are often incomplete, so some things must be sought by slowly browsing the original records—now done chiefly with microfilmed copies.

The story that emerged from our quest was clear. The legend of Sally Hemings as the slave mistress of Thomas Jefferson was a fabrication. Almost certainly the story originated with a distant cousin (David Meade Randolph) on the other side of the political spectrum (a Federalist), who also had been involved in a dispute over two entangled estates (Richard Randolph's and John Wayles's). The slanderous tales would strike first at Thomas Jefferson and then Congressman John Wayles Eppes (both Democratic Republicans). It is hard to assess the motivation of Thomas Jefferson in firing David Meade Randolph as marshal of Virginia. Jefferson sought the job for Randolph, but upon his election to president, he fired Randolph within a very few weeks. We simply cannot answer whether the firing of Randolph related

Preface

more to the rumored jury-packing or the legal maneuvers tied to the estates of John Wayles and Colonel Richard Randolph. When the sons of Richard Randolph refused to take responsibility for his debts, some of those debts were transferred to Jefferson and his fellow brothers-in-law. And those debts were large. But Jefferson was a zealot in the area of principled government, and it does seem likely that David Meade Randolph was simply one among many Federalists who were fired for what the Jeffersonian Republicans considered malfeasance of duty in pressing for partisan political gain.

In doing the research on this subject, we found a great deal of unanticipated information about John Wayles, father-in-law of Thomas Jefferson. Briefly described in the past as a wealthy slave dealer, the plentiful data on this much-maligned man demonstrated a different person. We have included a rather lengthy portrait of John Wayles, because he is at the center of this story, and the information on his life and activities has not been presented prior to this time. The "SALLY" story was a footnote to the history of Thomas Jefferson, a Founding Father of the United States of America. John Wayles had been simply a footnote to a footnote, but he is also an example of the rising middle class of the developing nation. We found no evidence of John Wayles holding any significant office in colonial Virginia. Yet he did live in Virginia for 33 years and made his own small contributions to the daily life of his times.

The place of John Wayles in the Wetmore/Hemings story of 1873 was prominent. If Wayles were indeed the father of Sally Hemings, then she was the half-sister of Jefferson's wife. This notion had led to many speculations about the relationship of Jefferson and Sally Hemings based on a "half-sister" idea. Some commentators suggested that Sally was more attractive to Jefferson because she resembled her "half-sister," while others said Sally Hemings, her siblings, and her children were accorded special privileges because of the "half-sister" relationship, rather than some long-term affair between Jefferson and Hemings. The late Douglass Adair speculated on these theories. Adair made something of a specialty in history of debunking the errors and myths. He never published his essay on the "SALLY" story, though it was published posthumously. (Douglass Adair, *Fame and the Founding Fathers*, ed. Trevor Colbourn, Indianapolis: Liberty Fund, 1998.) One of the cornerstones of Adair's pending assessment of this situation had been the statements of both Isaac Jefferson and Madison Hemings that John Wayles was the father of Sally Hemings. Isaac Jefferson painted lively pictures of persons he knew. But Isaac specifically noted "folks said" that some of the Hemings children were "old Mr. Wayles," thus reporting the newspaper slander of Isaac's time, rather than the detailed personal observations which characterized most of his account of life at Monticello. Madison Hemings never explicitly stated any sources—though implying many, he never was quoted as saying, "my Mother told me," or "my Grandmother said." According to Thomas Jefferson Randolph (through biographers Randall and Parton), the newspapers of the day circulated at Monticello and many people there had read those outlandish stories in the newspapers of 1802-1805. If Douglass Adair had access to the additional information that is available today, he might have completed and then actually published a much different article. We simply found no hints of John Wayles's being involved in such a relationship, and we found strong, though not incontrovertible, evidence against it. We hope that Adair would have been pleased with our work at discovering the truth regarding these matters through diligent research and a bit of "detective work."

Rebecca L. McMurry
James F. McMurry, Jr.
Edinburg, Virginia
July 2001